LEARN ENGLISH
As a Second Language For Beginners. (ESL) - Vol 1
By: Akanksha Massey

Copyright © 2025

Akanksha Massey

ALL RIGHTS RESERVED. NO part of this book may be reproduced or transmitted in any form by any means, electronic or mechanical, including photocopying and recording, or by any information storage and retrieval system, except as may be expressly permitted in writing from the author.

ISBN: Number

Published by:

www.owlpublishers.com

360 S Market St, San Jose, CA 95113,

United States.

Printed in the United States of America

Table of Content

Greeting People 1

Introducing / Introduction 1

Goodbye 1

Consideration 2

Appearance 2

Family Members 2

Assistance / Help 2

Parts of Body 3

Vocabulary 4

Simple Conversation Starters 6

Past Singular Questions 6

Past Plural Questions 6

Tenses 8

Simple Present 9

Negative Sentences (Not / Never) 9

Perfect Tenses 10

Perfect Tenses 11

Questions 12

Time or Place 13

Contracted Forms 14

Three Forms of Verbs 15

Verb Forms Table 15

Plural Nouns 16

Singular Nouns 16

Pronouns 17

Examples / Pronouns 17

Assessment Test I 18

Assessment Test II 21

About The Author 23
Book Description 24

Greeting People

- Hello / Hi (any time)
- Good morning (before 12 o'clock)
- Good afternoon (after 12 o'clock)
- Good evening (after 5 o'clock)

Introducing / Introduction

- My name is _____
- What is your name?
- Who are you?
- I am _____
- How do you do? (formal)
- Nice to meet you!
- Pleased to meet you!
- Nice to see you!
- Nice to see you again!

Goodbye

- Bye
- See you
- Goodbye
- See you later
- See you soon!
- Good night

Consideration

- How are you?
- Fine thank you
- Very well
- I am okay.

- What's wrong with you?
- I am sick.
- I am tired.

Appearance

- I am _____
- You are _____

- He is _____
- She is _____

Tall, Small, Young, Old, Slim, Fat, Handsome, Beautiful

Family Members

- Father / Mother / Parents / Child / Children / Son / Daughter / Brother / Sister
- Grandfather / Grandmother / Grandson / Granddaughter
- Uncle / Aunt / Husband / Wife
- Father-in-law / Mother-in-law / Brother-in-law / Sister-in-law

Assistance / Help

- Can I help you?
- May I help you?
- What can I do for you?

Parts of Body

Body Parts	
Arm	Eye
Chest	Hand
Elbow	Finger
Foot	Thumb
Head	Ears
Eyes	Nose
Mouth	Stomach
Hands	Heel
Feet	Toe nail
Toes	Cheek

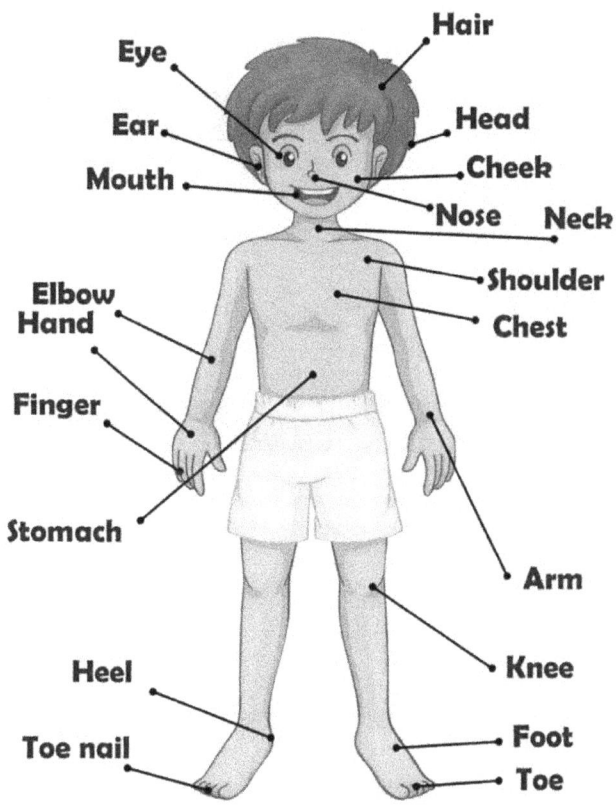

Vocabulary

Days of the Week	
Monday	Tuesday
Wednesday	Thursday
Friday	Saturday
Sunday	

Months	
January	February
March	April
May	June
July	August
September	October
November	December

Colors	
Red	Yellow
Black	White
Pink	Blue
Green	Brown
Orange	

Fruits	
Apple	Mango
Banana	Orange
Pineapple	Kiwi
Grapes	Pomegranate
Strawberry	Cherry
Blueberry	Peach
Watermelon	Plum
Papaya	Pear

Singular	Plural
Man	Men
Pen	Pens
Dog	Dogs
Fish	Fish
Cup	Cups
Book	Books
Car	Cars

Simple Conversation Starters

Nancy: Hi/Hello, how are you?

Sam: I'm fine/well. Thank you!

Sam: How are you?

Sam: What is your name? I am Sam.

Nancy: My name is Nancy.

Sam: Where do you live?

Nancy: I live in NYC.

Sam: What do you do?

Nancy: I am a teacher.

Past Singular Questions

- Was he there? (Person)
- Was she there?
- Was Sam sick?
- Was Nancy sick?
- Was I there?
- Was it old? (Non-person)
- Was it sick?
- Was it hungry?

Past Plural Questions

- Were they there? (Persons/People)
- Was I there?

Words that Sound Similar but Have Different Meanings

Accept **Means** Take
Except **Means** All but This

Hear **Means** Sound
Here **Means** Place

Hour **Means** Time
Our **Means** Belongs to us

One **Means** 1
Won **Means** Winning

It's **Means** It is
Its **Means** Belonging to it

You're **Means** You are
Your **Means** Belonging to you

Then **Means** What comes after
Than **Means** Comparing

Too **Means** Also; excessive
Two **Means** 2

Plane **Means** Flies in the sky
Plain **Means** Ordinary

Tenses

\multicolumn{2}{c}{**Past Tense**}	
I	Was / Were
He She It	Was
You We They	Were
\multicolumn{2}{c}{**Present Tense**}	
I	Am
He She It	Is
You We They	Are
\multicolumn{2}{c}{**Future Tense**}	
I	Will / Shall
He She It	Will
You We They	Will

Simple Present

Affirmative

Examples:

- I am a student.
- You are wise.
- The sun rises in the east.
- I play football.
- I smoke.

Negative Sentences (Not / Never)

- You do not work hard.
- Shiela does not sing well.
- He does not play.
- I am not blind.
- You are not rich.

Perfect Tenses

Present Perfect Tense	
I	Have
He She It	Has
You We They	Have
Past Perfect Tense	
I	Had
He She It	Had
You We They	Had
Future Perfect Tense	
I	Will have
He She It	Will have
You We They	Will have

Perfect Tenses

Present Perfect		Past Perfect		Future Perfect	
I	Have	I	Had	I	Will have
He	Has	You	Had	You	Will have
She	Has	He	Had	He	Will have
It	Has	She	Had	She	Will have
We	Have	It	Had	It	Will have
They	Have	We	Had	We	Will have
		They	Had	They	Will have

Questions

Present Plural Questions	
Are you okay?	People
Are they coming home?	
Are we going?	
Present Singular Questions	
Is he okay?	Person
Is she going?	
Is it working?	Non-person
Future Singular Questions	
Will he jump?	Person
Will she play?	
Will it work?	Non-person
Future Plural Questions	
Will they come over?	People
Will you tell them to come over?	
Will it work?	Non-person
Question Forms	
What?	Simple
Where?	
When?	
How?	
Who?	

Time or Place
words expressing nearest in

Direct	Indirect
Now	Then
This	That
These	Those
Ago	Before
This	That
Last day/year	The previous day/year
Next week/year	The following week/year
The day after tomorrow	In two days' time
Today	That day
Tomorrow	The next day / following day
Yesterday	The previous day / the day before
Last night	The previous night
Next week	The following week
A year ago	A year before / Previous year
The day before yesterday	Two days before
Come	Go

Positive	Negative
Open the door	Do not open the door
Come here	Do not come here
Sit outside	Don't sit outside
Let him sleep	Don't let him sleep
Do your work	Don't do your work
Stop eating	Don't stop eating

Contracted Forms	
is not	isn't
are not	aren't
was not	wasn't
were not	weren't
has not	hasn't
have not	haven't
had not	hadn't
do not	don't
does not	doesn't
did not	didn't
cannot	can't
could not	couldn't
should not	shouldn't
will not	won't
would not	wouldn't

Examples:

- You can't go = You cannot go
- I won't go there = I will not go there
- She does not say much = She doesn't say much
- He is not here = He isn't here
- They are not coming = They aren't coming

Three Forms of Verbs
Types of Forms

- Past / Present / Future
- Yesterday / Today / Tomorrow

Verb Forms Table

Present (1st)	Past (2nd)	Past Participle (3rd)	Present Participle
Act	Acted	Acted	Acting
Advise	Advised	Advised	Advising
Allow	Allowed	Allowed	Allowing
Ask	Asked	Asked	Asking
Attack	Attacked	Attacked	Attacking
Beat	Beat	Beaten	Beating
Become	Became	Become	Becoming
Break	Broke	Broken	Breaking
Call	Called	Called	Calling
Cast	Cast	Cast	Casting
Clean	Cleaned	Cleaned	Cleaning
Die	Died	Died	Dying
Dry	Dried	Dried	Drying
Eat	Ate	Eaten	Eating

Plural Nouns

I / We / You / They

Singular Nouns

He / She / It / Father / Mother

Rules for negatives:

- Use "do not" with (I, We, You, They)
- Use "does not" with (He, She, It)

Use of "is"
Present

Examples:

- He **is** my father.
- She **is** my friend.
- It **is** working.

Plural / Present	
We	Are
They	Are
You	Are

Examples:

- We **are** friends.
- They **are** playing.

Pronouns

	Single Person	
Singular Person	He Him	Boy Man Male
	She Her	Girl Women Female
Singular	It	Non-human

Examples / Pronouns
Personal Pronouns Table

Person	Subject	Object	Possessive
First Person	I, we	me, us	my, mine, our, ours
Second Person	you	you	your, yours,
Third Person	he, she, it, they	him, her, it, them	his, her, hers, its, their, theirs

Assessment Test I

Fill in the Blanks (is / am / are / my / I / his / her / this)

1. I _____ a student.
2. _____ name is (Your name).
3. She _____ my friend.
4. They _____ friends.
5. You _____ my sister.
6. What _____ you doing?
7. A bird _____ small.
8. This _____ a small bird.
9. My father _____ a doctor.
10. _____ name is (for a boy).
11. _____ name is (for a girl).
12. _____ my friend (boy).
13. _____ my friend (girl).
14. This _____ my cat.
15. _____ is my dog.
16. _____ I talking?
17. _____ you eating?
18. _____ they sleeping?
19. _____ TV working?
20. _____ is not reading. (boy)
21. _____ is going out. (girl)
22. That _____ my pencil.
23. You _____ not sleeping.
24. They _____ playing.
25. Am _____ late?

26. This _____ my book?

27. That _____ your dog?

28. Am _____ leaving?

Answers for Assessment Test I

1. am
2. My
3. is
4. are
5. are
6. are
7. is
8. is
9. is
10. His
11. Her
12. He is
13. She is
14. is
15. This
16. Am
17. Are
18. Are
19. Is
20. He
21. She
22. is
23. are
24. are
25. I
26. is
27. is
28. I

Assessment Test II
Fill in the Blanks (is / are / it / he / she)

1. He _____ my father.
2. She _____ your sister.
3. It _____ working.
4. You _____ sleeping.
5. They _____ playing.
6. We _____ learning.
7. _____ is a dog.
8. _____ is my friend.
9. _____ is my sister.
10. _____ is my brother.
11. _____ my teacher.
12. _____ my father.
13. They _____ eating.

Answers for Assessment Test II

1. He is my father.
2. She is your sister.
3. It is working.
4. You are sleeping.
5. They are playing.
6. We are learning.
7. It is a dog.
8. He/She is my friend.
9. She is my sister.
10. He is my brother.
11. She/He is my teacher.
12. He is my father.
13. They are eating.

About The Author

I, Akanksha Massey, started working part-time as a school teacher at a very young age, along with other jobs, all while attending school/college myself. A few years ago, I was hired to teach ESL online to international students of all ages and grades/standards, from 3rd-grade/standard students to post-graduate M.A. students from various countries. I always received excellent reviews from each student and their parents.

The reason for writing this book was that I saw the students were not enjoying the ESL books/lessons provided by the school because they were too advanced in vocabulary and didn't help them while they were starting to learn English as a second language (ESL). Thus, my suggestion to change the book's format was approved by the CEO for international students. This book is VOL.1 for those who are trying and want to begin to learn English as a second language.

During this time, while I was teaching, I obtained a license for Loan Signing and Notary of California as well from Pierce College Extension in California. I have also been given a Certificate of Achievement in the field of education and teaching. Recently, I was hired yet again as a highly qualified teacher.

My pursuit is to make ESL as easy and fun as possible with this book.

Book Description

This Vol. 1 ESL book is designed to make learning English as a second language easy and simple for beginners of all ages. Step by step, it will help you begin to communicate in English as you start to understand the simple lessons provided in this book. It can also be useful for school curriculum purposes.

I wish you happy learning!

There are individual lessons provided as well for beginners, should you wish to learn through online classes. This is additionally helpful if you are Indian, speak only Hindi, and wish to learn ESL.

If you would like to get one-on-one coaching or the online sessions, you can connect with us at: learningeslwithakanksha@gmail.com.

www.ingramcontent.com/pod-product-compliance
Lightning Source LLC
Chambersburg PA
CBHW060623070426
42449CB00042B/2479